A Girl Who Was His House

To Emma
Love from
Sarah-Jean
S.

Praise for *A Girl Who Was His House*

"Sarah-Jean Krahn's second book of poetry is a startling collection where meaning arrives at the cusp of word-shifts and mind-shifts to shock, surprise, reveal, and simply tell the tale of a girl who thrives in the cracks of God's-and-man's sidewalks. A Girl Who Was His House *is experimental poetry at its decadent best—eerily political, sharply responsible, tearful and fun-filled. Krahn is a gift to Canadian Literature."*

-Clara A. B. Joseph, author
of *The Face of the Other*

"A Girl Who Was His House *sweeps us behind a turtle shell of piercing, witty barbs, a map of 'her education at home.' An insidious schooling where he 'watched you hours.' Sarcasm, small recourse for the powerless, overwhelms 'in the numbness of his medicine.' Still, Sarah-Jean Krahn, the poet, resuscitates and shows us what resilience and braveness means."*

-Elaine Woo, author of
Put Your Hand in Mine and
Cycling with the Dragon

"A Girl Who Was His House *continues Krahn's relentless linguistic and narrative deconstruction of the abject (first begun in* Weed Apologue*), in which the alienation wrought on the latent female self by the forces of patriarchy leads to a riotous reckoning between the imagination's take on desire and connection and that of language as it seals and unseals ever-changing bodies that resist easy definition."*

-Emily Cargan, writer,
researcher, and educator

"A Girl Who Was His House *is ferocious, vulnerable, and bold—examining the female experience in bursts of words that not only challenge predictable syntax but deliver language like an avenging angel opening her wings to sound and sense. Sometimes the poems hit like a punch to the gut, sometimes they whisper, grieve, protest, indict. And always the passion of the poems centers in the female body, its beauty and perils, and rage at how it has been violated by male domination and abuse."*

-Jan Worth-Nelson,
author of *Night Blind*

"Sarah-Jean Krahn's A Girl Who Was His House *repurposes the female body and the domestic in a way that cannot be appropriated by patriarchy. She does indeed, 'Reclaim this space from your misery,' in a powerful and innovative articulation of female subjectivity and resistance."*

-Katherine Davis, author
of *The Anger Poems*

"Sarah-Jean Krahn's rich, lyrical collection confronts living and longing with a playful danger that dances across the page like a knife's edge."

-Nic Custer, author of
Nothing Works, Everyone Labors

Praise for *Weed Apologue*

"Stunning, extraordinary and highly accomplished. This is the sort of work that people will be talking about in the future as a key work of Canadian literature."

-Emily Cargan, writer,
researcher, and educator

"Krahn's poetry condemns Canadian colonialism and its impact on Indigenous women and the environment while weaving language in a way that cannot be anything but like a so-called weed: insistent, seemingly effortless, hardy, and, ultimately, beautiful."

-Terrence Abrahams,
author of *a wish*

A Girl Who Was His House

Sarah-Jean Krahn

GOTHIC FUNK PRESS
Flint, Michigan

GOTHIC FUNK PRESS

gothicfunkpress.com

Flint, Michigan

A GIRL WHO WAS HIS HOUSE

Edited by **Elisabeth Blair**

Designed by **Sam Perkins-Harbin**

Illustrated by **Sarah-Jean Krahn** and **Jeff Watt**

ISBN: 978-0-9899202-8-5

Printed in the United States of America

10 9 8 7 6 5 4 3 2 1
First Edition

I must put this away,—
he hates to have me
write a word.

—Charlotte Perkins Gilman,
"The Yellow Wallpaper"

For Ewe

The poems in this collection
are collages of the found.

Dance around them,
but purposefully.

Contents

A Tea Party in the Co-op Parking Lot

or,

The strong arms and soft belly of a gentlewitch incite summer sunlight in her brewding maiden's cheeks.

"You have such a striking
face, my dear; no need for make-up
a-

t'all!"
thinner
all the time
eyes trample
head and neck

a
contract

"The only thing I did every day
was swab my cheeks
with chamomile tea."

and stood-alone

hand-thrown

"(Of course maybe all
you have to
do is *smile* . . . !)"

(. . . For him.)

Eat right;
Avoid the sun;
Look at your stupid face!

Slough the dead
Bikini;

It's one less thing to be shy about.

"Thirty years I
was with him, you

know" survive/ors
navel corps:

on lazy evenings
bestir yourself

in the bath of bubble
Pledge

not to make-up
not to drink-up but

(clutter your frown with boils!)

Bodily bedtime
autonomy:

push all you've ever
known
to squall.

Narcissus may be mistaken
for Chamomile. "My dear,
not all abuse is physical."

You can find chamomile in the most
unexpected of places; for instance, she
thrives in the cracks of sidewalks.

I place the double-paper bagged produce gently
on her coup/e's passenger—

Late

at home I dump
a box of tea bags
in the tub

soak yellow

and shirk
the relentless
phone.

Her German name is
alles zutraut

meaning capable
of anything.

menarche

pronounced

like
anarchy

Cotton, Dry

P.U.
cubicle
unkempt lock

unruly lip
a monarch
migration

popular,
if lite,

in the lite rare
arts

11-year-old
loosens her belt

says "We are
just as

able

as men"

I pump

back and forth on the neighbour kid's
red swing-set

the crescent
cradles me
cups me
holds me taught

in stinct-
“ur
on the rag”
he says

not
pushing
only
flinging

bits of dog
shit into my lap
face

I try to spit
on him I spit
on my lap in
stead

He was the only boy I could stand

up to

now he had never paid me any
head except as the understanding
friend but now that his girlfriend danced
with some other
loser he wanted to grind his thing

against me   we   all
slept in the same bed that he—

                    the night he—

but that
night he just spooned her

strawberry
backaches
baked-in-the-sand

books ooze
with thickredfoldedhalfwaysjam

(It was messy.)

(I had to explain to my parents.)

men's
truth
psychs

le
man
in la moon;

o, pause!

one small step
for manners

...then, she transformed into a B-U-T-full BUTTERFLY!

Vandalism

or,

Lovemaps of p~~ed~~sychiatric women
on the brink of disorderly conduct.

However, when I finally got The Point,
my lover only lived up to parental standards
until he proved he was totally unPointed.

Lovemaps

~~*L*~~*over*~~*naps*~~
so quickly?

My dad does not all
-ow us to learn geography
with such considerable Frankness, as—

Something Queer is Going On!
by Elizabeth Levy

I adore the twin-igmas
of Jill and Gwen,
have to tell you all
about them.

Something smooth, and ~~fulf~~ill~~ing~~,
and then? and then!—

"Queer is when a boy gets his period."
The End?
No. "Queer is you thinking the girl's on top."
The.
Queer is I am her boy.
End.
But then—

Something Strange
is Going On in the very next title
no longer Queer but
still

Friends:

Annetiques, brakeables,
to be ~~lo~~ok~~ed at~~,
never ~~t~~ouch~~ed~~!

Who~~Mul~~ligan?
You-lligan
and Her-lligan
in the backseat of the van again

getting driven to Babysitters' Ed.

The rest of us make awk
-ward intercourse while moms
leer to the rear
-view mirror.

Later, my other she ejaculates with laughter
when I say ejacu(late) in a manner of ~~s-~~peeking.

I try to turn it off while we're in the trailer,
bedbouncing down dirt roads, one axle.

But the van-dollism of the empty house clinched it.

You'd never meet the Rigid Criteria
for member(ship) in The Babysitters' Club.

And I was bare-ly
~~all-~~owed   to Baby

Sit.

(~~Queerly~~ Strangely enough, I re-
member sitting
on the floor of my clothes
-et while I list
-end to mothers gossip about you.)

You're casual
and do-it

-yourself,
a shiny ace,

the answer
to family values,
safety from deviant behaviour.

I was going to hell when I went
to church with you.

Still.
Friends.

Because you shared my love
of mis~~t~~eries,

and the purity
of our ~~r~~elation~~ship~~
remained locked

(even while my favourite game was
Runaways).

It's weird that I met you in church instead of her.
I wrote my Language Arts provincial all about you.

The Gooey Mess began
when you yelled through
the phone at my father:
"We're murdering her with a pick
-axe, oh my god!"

But the leering figure in the doorway
wasn't you.

Perhaps He exploded because you took
His Name in Vain?

Never would I get to explore your
Foul Mouth.

He drove me/The Point home;
you, Partner of every god and goddess,
drove under a bus
and came out
the other side.

Grades Too Low,
Apt to Skip Class,
Pulled Out of School for—?

Maybe a miraculously pregnant woman
-lover!:

She III: *I ran into Donna ~~and her girlfriend~~ the other day.*

"She's acting like you're her boyfriend,"
Moms
said Pointedly.

Then

they made me break

up

with

you.

Thanks for the Invitation

or,

Not dumbing down a reconstructed splinter of the cute-forces genre, where the forefather coupler watches me grow, and other really creepy things.

Has anyone ever seen that Dr. Phil
with the inordinately dangerous
relatable girl character?

The one utterly practiced
at manipulating temptation
in sympathetic adult men?

The one whose Hugs-and-Bunny-Kisses
punctuate Mister Honeymoon till he succumbs
to the common germs of her security blanket?

The fluffy little lamb who persecutes
the Guardian of Truth and fosters
her own negative motor pathways?

Attention Whore.

(Babies are Legion.)

The moment he arrives,
"What a precious snap of a daughter!"

This posh pensioner,
the smartest person in the room,
jovial, loudly laughing,
lifetimes lost in gracious interaction.

But such a strange relationship
favours silence by the sink:
pat-pat-there-there,
an unexpected embrace

Pleasant to the touch,
playful swipe,
vigor heave;
salivary glands unite

Whole body dancing,
shirt soaking wet,
"Jabberwocky loves you,"
a familiar effect

(We can see the top of her head.
His re-touch ploy engulfs
her entire chemical imbalance.)

The lustful shrivel
does him proud.

There is no such thing as
well-intentioned
munchkin-muffining
without permission.

The author herself,
accommodating the absurdity of the above,
now transfers to the more subtle problems:

  An "accidental touch" in the elevator,
  unsolicited "kindness" following small talk,
  a genius in sculpture when she tries to leave.

  his Gothic Raygun thrusts against her solace,
  his Phantasmal Slider floats behind her skin, and
  his Mind Projection scans her schematics
  while all their Prehistoric Scruples prosecute her
    scream.

Trousers quant-defy rationalization,
her own niche portrayed as hypersensitive.

Associating them with criminality
represents a Radical and Aggressive heuristic.

And you sure can't talk back!
Writing an 11-page letter is nagging,
Correcting their grammar is judgybitch.

Any girl on their Kill Screen
is the humbled recipient
of periscope scum

who otherwise can't have
sex

or pay the bills.

Meanwhile, her editors discuss the worst
vote they've ever cast;

there's nothing breezy about printing Cupcake Fascism—
I mean, Feminism—

Explorations in the Tension.

The proximate positioning of a hug.

A sad, yet beautiful egg,

she has to be in the same room.

Has anyone ever seen that Oprah?

The one where our worst thoughts and acts
wedded a structure of bad
thoughts-quashing?

The one with the invented statistics
finally supplanted?

The one where you removed your pacifier?

Ate your veggies?

Herded your theological belly defect out of the closet
for good?

Comment is free;
mentor your younger self with gleam

—Full Stop—

You need to see
the Phallusy.

Reclaim this space from your misery.

Woman Messages

or,

The shallow breaths (not to mention bare breasts) of a cranky sexpot, lonely for allies late in the afternoon, but *not* under the influence of contraceptive pills.

initial thought to
publish whoop(s)ie

—a softer world!
too good a sense!—

erroneously asserts
the gazer shall
                    restrain himself when shirt spills guts.

first time in public
buttons pop

cleavage naïve
as gazer fades

my fashion secret
conference turncoats

future dead friends.

thirsteen
whoreteen
fitsteen

sexteen

crycryteen

sateen
painteen
slavety

no uncertain terms
those damning words
peel away humaniteen

a D-list of no-nos
to the nth degree
bloodyshame
beatdownsane
to truly be free

complimentariteen
"pure at heart"

honors to a tightlipteen
with "character-smarts"

giveawayherfavorsteen
"this bitch is a steal"

twink(l)ie dominatreen
"let that frosty skank squeal"

Give Mammary Some Pedigree!
foreplays my bosom mission

But my patrons sizzle limply
leering with flavourless derision.

Now they gang-chew me out!:

"No justification for her toxin—
sexual literacy talkin

yes-means-yes
va-va-vagary

and of course those fugly lungs."

So,
deletions and revisions.
I must shake them from my body.

My biggest wardrobe failure
—a huge rack of tries

but devastation to those I love—
dies from complications.

shimmy

sin

ashamed

I was a teenage dinner.

She has lost herself.

Unsure of the official rules,
she checks her corset.

Her follow button has broken.
It's not enough to cream her.
She never defends herself,
just massages her trial lyrics,
so that a few girls, perhaps, won't help but feel bad, and

break out their topless party-hats!

in an attempt

to moonwalk

past

the whole

“whore” aspect.

Her monthly sweat approaches.
See her shaking. Friend requests batter.
Likes: the headlock delusion.
Notifications: waves of percussion.
Comments: poison waterfall.
The “little slut's” grieving?

Never noticed.

No Privacy... but COOKIES!

or,

Given that it's hard to fight with fists in a jar, a couple in love squeezes through a chasm as the classic result of crusty Raggedy Androcentrism.

One Big Happy Family
all ferment on each other
in Fungal Emotional Ventures
and Sexual/Leavening Events.

Peanut Pets
Pecan Saints
Picky Brittle

Each pocket-sized person
a pocky molecule
in the Popovary Galaxy.

I'm yours/
you're mine
without the hassle of wires

Multi-pass
slide
through parallel
beds

for each crumb of uncomfortable kindness.

Take these desserts
and plunder a third
gourmet leftover of stranglers
lucky
to pulse
such

S/table
Bonds.

Gentle,
delectable,
soft.

Can chinchillas kill?

From 1 million

to despair

They're about
to murder
each other!

Rainbow braided horns

encrypt

their beaks' unscripted

bleats

Preparation from beyond the crypt.

The recipe for grief.

From first morsel to the final stitch,
Play-epaulettes spellbind lips.

Jam-	Fasten their Blinkers
Torte-	Fashion their Pow/dered Cheeks
Gingersnap-Fash	their Sleeping Souls
Sugar-Burn	their Serviettes.
Good-People	scrape flesh
Over-Pampered	melty pelts.

Bedeck their biscuits
upon crisply handmade silk.

(*The quality is scrumptious!*)

(*Irreverent, even!*)

(Butters and other body parts
Encrust our secret purses.)

Happily Devoured After!

Must preserve proof by freezer
for safety in numbness.

A real
treat/ise.

The union of thinking thieves.

(For just two players

Or S'More.)

As many tasteless concoctions as possible.

Snicker and Doodle
Pfeffer and Neusse
Aspic and Jelly
Humble and Pie

A.
B.
C.

Or E.?

I know this list can get O so sticky.

So X.

EACH. OTHER.

(I love this step.)

In a searing twist
with my bathroom in my backpack,

Bereft of wastel and where to go.

~~(But,~~
~~that's just how the cookie crumbles!)~~

Seduction

or,

Being ground up and in the freezer as she was, her nerves were shot, and she couldn't help but wallow in the Old School sexism of it all.

He said:
"I like my women"

women's powder and finery,
the art of the tease,
the dance,
women.

Beautiful women . . .

Need I say more?

He said:
"my women like"

shiny granite, marble,
honey, nectar,
time

to heat their superfluous lees . . .

Maybe it needs to be made explicit.

He said:
"women like"

to be picked and cherished,
to caramelize in the sun,
to warble through a filter,

delivered from the frigg—,

I'll clarify.

He said:
"like I like"

a slit in the skirt
a skittering mound
a big lunch and a corporate paycheck

Free Shipping!

and a bit of an online garboil
over

coffee.

Coffee, the metonymic date.

"And where do you go on your dates?"

An elevated surface consisting of a mattress
and a base
(with debate over Pickton's pig-grounds.)

(He said he couldn't walk across them
without installing a tourist village.)

He said:
"coffee"
"*my* coffee"

Slack water?
Shallow?
Memory and thought swirls too
weak to

Stand up!

"And what do you do on your dates?"

He instructs the ritual grounds to slumber.
Impales aimlessly the softest of spots.
He says to repay the favour he's owed
but neglects to rouse her
from torpor.

In this hush his women render:

the "fat chick distributing free hand jobs,"
the "yeti lurking the community pool,"
the "happy but headstrong girl's buckingteeth,"
and nine more one-woman shows.

Nitty-gritties
Freezer-burn.

—let me make it plain:

"I like my women like I like my coffee: ground up
and in the freezer."

And I really like to complain.

Girl, Oddly Worn

or,

Gone are the days of the grape-feeding girls; we're all mental hygienists now.

Being in the rubbing years,
her curiosity was capable
of exultation.

Human and
priestess,
mounted

have finishes
finishes finishes

exquisite g(u)ilt to the elated.

Emptiness shimmies the pyramid's crown.

Relations.
Remains.

Transgression.

If the professor followed form
tightly tucked himself in object—

artifactual
insemination.

The text—
a silence—
servant-girl of desire—
mines only degrees,

plates polished intrigue.

She.

Through mournings,
one She trembles,

startles his corridor
itches his abdomen
expels his production

from its easement

pitiless,
penniful

forces his dwelling from its dressing
with her unde(r)serving subjectivity

and undeserting uneasiness

Her century into witchcraft
crimson farmhouse
femininity

pierces secrets
stitches sack
throbs blessed ingot bliss.

Panoplied hysteric
doubles bitten-off words.

This hysteria and

well,

heredity
—mysterical liars—

fear

what lies above.

She'll.

Lie in
the pool.

Fold her dearest
diamond into
her pocket.

Secrete.

Symptom-atology of an Impostor

- you call yourself an instructor
  when the dept. classifies you as a T.A.;

- you fret over how to pretend you
  know what you're talking about but
  fifty minutes fly by when you talk about

- Feminist Theory
  is too subjective they say;
  Queer Theory is as point-
  less as "Working-at-McDonald's Theory"

- which is technically probably what
  constitutes Marxist, but you
  weren't the instructor then and

- to the queer question you
  probably would've said "No"
  while philosophizing about how isn't
  everyone, really, queer?;

- a student informs you
  of the women's dance this weekend,
  asks: "You are queer, aren't you?" to which you
  reply "Um . . . yes?"

- you're not a dancer or a
  crowd-pleaser and no one
  dances with you; silly
  to think maybe *she* would take you
  to the floor and show you how it's done;
  student instructs teacher; maybe they all
  know you're a fraud in your faux
  hawk and camo pants; equal
  to the het clubs your best
  pal used to drag you to.
  "Oh, I thought you two
  were, you know,
  together"

- a theory you cannot admit;
  think, "She's not my type";

  but at the long-awaited news you're bi, her response: "I'm

  unavailable."

The Impersonal is Poclitical

(Let's get the name
-calling out
of the way first.)

"The Virgin Queen":
Independent.
Feminist.
Cliterati.

Female utility.

Imagine trying to explain to someone what it
feels like to sneeze or yawn

or to hear the screams of someone having her head
hacked off.

With the help of a razor or knife many girls die [. . .] throughout
their whole lives.

(It is not the book that cuts the clitoris, but its interprettytions aid
and abet the mutilation.)

Clitoris Not A Must

"Thank God! Apparently
the long tearanny of the clitoris is coming
to its end, dearest.

If you axe me, if you want sex
as a mechanical act, you want
to put on a clitoris.

For a while there we were moving
toward a period
of you-biquitous, cyborg frenzology[!]"

(Oh, honey.

I feel your frustration.

My clitoris couldn't find herself

if she ate

prayed

loved.)

The Man-ual

A dense 200-plus pages of instruction with some
clear line drawings to illustrate!

Origins
and
erogenous zones!

Your eyes,
their pleasure!

Doctor's orders!

You will find yourself thinking, "Hmm,
so that's where they come from."

This book is now available for the first time
on DVD and Blu-Ray:

Bigger.
Longer.
And uncut.

Runaway Beaver Cut Off at Pass:
Man Fractures Arms

Not winning when it comes to detached lower lips?

Dual-use items (such as the labia
minora/majora)

can be used to manufacture arms
for military catch-&-release tactics:

cotton swabs,
rubber gloves,
and scopes of various sizes.

(Please note:

Clitoridectomy requires the removal of the entire
regi   me

"   on

ME.)

However, if you enjoy it,

YOU
are going to
he[ck]!

Out of (the Bush) and Back
to the American Cities

The next patient will require general anesthesia
    and a fish hook.

Imagine the woman's quiet desperation
as Get Off-icials perforate
the fibrous capsule [. . . and] project
into   the spaces

Noise.

Then, on the floor of a dusty closet,
they stitch both sides of the organ back together

just as Gods
intended.

Clitoris Widely Known before Man's Discovery

Still, is often omitted
on anatomical diagrams
given students.

(Such as female neonates with nothing better to do.)

Sew,
Ex-cite.

Warning: Clitoral simulation
may pro-liferate
Gen-Exic earth defects.

(A clitoris, causitively stolen.)

Then
Excise.

Choice between 1,000s of Nervous Endings
Means Old Wives' Tails about to Be Published

Concealed.

The conflict has left
many internally displaced.

Visible!

She taught me to use this vibrator
in car jackings.

Biopunk.

Cultural relativism fails
to justify my pleasure.

I should be kissed,
and kissed often.

Cultish.

Kittenesque!
and wait for me

Ring the doorbell
to open the door.

A species of meat art?!

I am
an exorcism.
Sex.
Weird shit.

Women's passionate love affairs
with the clitoris outrage
the blades of razors or knives.

Gramarye

or,

Whatever happened to the Magic of our Monarchye—er—Dream of our Democracye, never before stopped by combat, xenophobia, or demagoguery, and, being so late in the operation, whatever happened to Sarah-Jean?

Spiderye

(The solving of the problem rests with the women.)

Tarantula spawn across Parliament Hill:
these tiny furry carrions are bringing forth a bill

so hurry on scurry on
so many bones to pick!

Fear-puffed balloons
uphold corroded roofs

while deep within the postbox
bulge the seering t(r)ooths

that puncture copper
guttle trusses
pulsate pupal guts

Tarantulae swarm through patriot halls:
against emblems, concessions,
White Paper flies

in the way of the screen

so much
blood

Symmetrye

A video plays against the mauve-eyed clouds above,
        In real time—
A woman, frail and white, more elderly over weeks,
        blind-folded, skin pulled tight to pale temples,
        shot once, in the head, to mark
        the fallen in the holy
        time of Ramadan.

A video plays up ahead in droves of chestnuts,
        Staticky, suppressed—
A man (boy?), limbs slumped aside (coy?),
        plays fucking dead
                        not dead (this Marines division said)
        Fucking Faking It, so blood-
        shot once, in the chest, just in case;

                Carry On.

Flatterye

Arms
welcome stamps

Carry-on
un(a)bashed

Soles
seep sement

Shimmer croons
mesmerize:
Soooooo romantic!

Neck/romantic:

why my sternum
is squelched

my squealing is
stumped

coxa-ed
over
uni(n)form/ed
shoulders
like a sac
of young

potatoes

Oratorye

Attention, attention.
Paging
Officer Te Ammo.

"Gramarye *is*.
Check my dictionarye.
Check your dictionarye.
Heed my oratorye.
Heed the Googlye!

Tell my sibling I love them;
this contaminancye
seeps deep into my drollerye

And my veins are the
marrower
for Your Excellencye

to creep
through and smother
all hopes of hard hungerye

I love her, I love them,
in a panic, I love that
Gramarye is, and—
Look out! There's one on me!"

Your post-flight
mission
awaits.

Burye

That was the year it became clear she had never been faking anything; the nothingness was true; the shot was only a needle drawing the blood that would be inexplicably found clear; yet still the sickness remained, and when the people tripped over it, they sounded the alarm.

“Yes, Sir, the war is going well. . . .

. . .

“Yes, we’re cracking down on the education of women.”

(We were having a conversation about birthdays.

About astrological signs, actually. And when your mum said yay Libras are so good you said not always. Your point being not that Libras are inherently bad, but that Libras aren't inherently good either.)

your play-
ground takes up

arms, flings sand
at fire, ferments;

space, left alone
at the park   to hang;

two-wheeling, a goal
for the school year

2 seconds later
slow puncture

—Stop.—

over there
you can't tell a leaf
from a half-dead turtle

unexplained trail of slime
flip-flops by the slide

glistens like an oyster's
shoelace-gazing act

the forest
drowns
in heavy gales,
vomits in the sand

your painstaking attention to detail
        trembles by the swings

"I have watched you hours."

bite-sized red bits

                    led into the woods.

space

air

your playground
hurtles earth

arms held high
tiny overalls or

spacesuit

?

carries turtle shells   mars
in need of hope—   on

growable

trace secretions
of slugs to spring-

board their cells into the future

last count of the species:
completely numb and few

so you pursue the sparkle
on one flip-flopped foot
into the snarl of brush

bed-and-bath parts
exposed

to Big Red Bits.

a smelling thing exits the body.

A circle was drawn on the

ground a round
the Man towards the end of his infant

Function Insufficient

came out evenly castrated
could not sit up
straight

forbidden to grow at the playground
tried to crawl under a pillow
to expire

you play
underground

forevermore flanked
by a hammer and flask

a zombie
a monk
a lackluster villain
the least biological risk

Even
after the fair-tale betrothal
to the Libra of your future.

Peaches

or,

A term of endearment for animals who prefer to be eaten.

The earwig proposes a thesis about circles:

There is no half.

Her tallest dancer tastes terrible
in music but in pants

it matters not what one spots there
so long as they sad her in bed.

She asks if I ever miss dick then giggles,
cunnilinguaes the pedicel of a peach

Not mine.

(Her dad thanks me for taking care of her.)

every dusk the saucers
dish my tender sill

i do not miss but
the bitter crib i thrill

The Guests slice each half
from clingstone ischia and grill

haft the tinder with a switch:
"Do we dare to eat a peach?"

the twig ill
with blossom rot

The manager chuckles at my imagination
promises the pomegranates will soon be in

because I often complain of the substandard produce
and the feeling of a bug in my hair

the peach's pale meat of dishwater smacks
and the pit splits long its hemisphere

laughs an earwig across the counter.

(My dad thanks you for taking care of me.)

I say goodbye as he scurries and
nibble the core's absinthe almond

my chosen dad's favourite fruit is the peach
warms the days of a defunct daughter
grafts a batch of ice cream pail

-fruit salad
melts in a grateful grin
in the numbness of his medicine

he may inhabit a mammoth peach
and bob the muddled creek

to meet you and me
and everyone
seems

to know

the josh
I don't get

so I titter
and nip
the tongue's pulp

I'm
Home.

When you shed your scalp's winter's coat
for the first time you call
yourself a fuzzy peach
and the endearment
beams

thrust into you
I can't stop my gaze
down at your blossoming face

but it's your fuzzy peaches I squeeze
every night the down
that I graze
with my
cheek
and
the
seam
where
I linger
even when your flue

crows the husks of bygone earwigs
who dared penetrate to the quick
of a tender

Peach

(I can't always
say goodbye, but
I will
spit them across the room

and nurture your
freestone
spine.)

Journal of Dead Bodies & Hidden Treasures

If, for the first time,

you've missed your own deadline
in a self-similar respect,

you may remain
unaware
of the subplots.

Women are often uninformed that
we may elicit pipeline
data as innocent pawns

to culturally-prescribed
femininity.

What follows might not be entirely
satisfactory or a just state
of affairs,

but control over information
release should be made
non-intrusive in the near future.

Day 24: began drinking ginger tea intermittently

Waves in certain directions
do not start to bleed;

Access to perfect isn't taught in school
even in the presence of crisis.

Until basic resources are decriminalized
and all combinations of sweat-proof return,

the coordination of ubiquitous webs
will syncopate with creative debate.

"Processing your request"
for much needed relief
from a fatally bad habit
compels.

"What problems are you having?"

Adaptations can improve control
over menstrual cyclicity and disable
the blows of bad medicine.

Some hope.

Day 29 through 32: drank ginger tea in earnest

First-fail. Must be rerun at some later time.

<u>Day 32 through 35:</u> 6000 mg Vit. C/day

Wait.
Morning.
Sickness. Dread.
Sleep. Laundry.
A bit of a scene.

Terminate. Argument.
Do a little research
to let yourself sleep. Again.

Type escape sequence:
Forbidden Grief.

Uncertainty has
to end.

Day 36: parsley pessary

Here's misstated evidence
of a new record!

I've tried a million little things
to get rid of what I thought.

I've inserted speculation
up my vasovagal gate,
prematurely overloaded
active rounds of coarse control.

I've anonymized data
on the spices and the pills,
decoded the best technique
for predicting modern style.

While traditional sources
disable trust-based context,
I've addressed my basket
in a firm but gentle way.

I've cooperated willingly.

I've meant fucking business.

I've selectively throttled my little hole
for a creamy self-delete.

I've forcefully

stopped

the execution.

goes to her cabinet and
removes the robust
architecture of a porcelain

bowl.

Keeping it?

Endometrial
f
l

o

o

o
o o
o
o o o
o . o o
o d o
o o

Among Friends

or,

The regulation of ribbon colours surrounds consent with resentment, and an unexpected trip to a super fun location promotes unnecessary treatment.

I've been having chest
pains.

Fortunately, those who choose to wear it
can afford access to a physician.

Capable of little intelligible dialogue
He instead pulls out
the pink rose
of my delicate feminine affectation.

"Your main/tertiary sexual characteristics
have likely rented sequins or stripes
on your princess party-favour cones!"

Philanthropy's assistant
with a half-and-half hitch
exposes a slight swelling:

"Do your impossibly undermined eye candies
accept the mission to pinpoint pink playgrounds?"

(Ha ha ha. Tuck.
In a messy hand.)

Now, emotional support:
"All different shapes and sizes,
in whole or in part,
can pass promptly to risk
paired with urgent need."

Apparently a door
knob had embedded
in my poor neglected tits.

I will never forget
the empowered folks,
laughing together,
revealing their scars

Like grace at a funeral.

Sisters, friends, neighbours,
they were talking without limitation:

"So much activity around here lately!"

"Her life is split"
"She looks nothing like you!"

Is it that obvious?

Fortunately, my chosen mom's easy on-and-off
repartees better outcomes
than my not-a-mouse inertia;

Her cultured satin floods
the room with global trust.

Hygiene decrees I forgo regular garments
for more appropriate facilities.

She compliments my slip-on frock
with its crisp plastic weave

My cheeky grin:
I'm sure the men enjoy this
cheerful singlet scarlet suit!

The women opine: "Actually,
the men are steered toward blue."

From then on I maintained polite distance.

The natural aesthetic of wood-panelled walls
counters the compulsorily pink
imaging machine.

Constant stimulation keeps
my shrunken puppets firm
in position as slightly zealous
chat distracts tool-lady:

"Low female literacy"
                    "A journey to inspire"
          "Education"
"A fairytale"
                    "A real live magical shawl!"

As for me,
the pre-press treatment,
though not perfect,
isn't brutal
                              —due to my lack of basic resources.

One might even say it
vanquished trepidation
and refreshed my angel heart!

                              (I'm a total ditz...)

Quietly and demurely sit back
against the blank-book sheet

Prevention is in progress.

This grand tea-time
has lost all its charm.

Sticky stains jacket
my tender French rabbits,

ballooned over
by tacky TP

—but BINGO!

A frustrating lack of faults found
in my adorable productions!

"However, if we don't run a more radical report,
your physician will hang me in public."

Corral my thoughts
with breathless gulps;
I'm sorry but I can't indulge

"A crucial move";
"Now please don't fuss";
wince even more;
no, please

I don't want;
efforts to block;
splayed index/middle fingers;

"I'm going to squeeze her";
"Distract her hands";
            They turn on her and count—

—Surprise hit on a *But I*— breast!—

A Giant
Pair

of Scissors.

In medical terms, a huge success:
The control to eradicate dread.

    But I've been having chest
    pains.

Lack of range of motion.
Reluctance or inability to ask.

Due to the radiation?   No.
There's no cross-clip on my crests.

    But I've been having chest pains.
    Because assaults persist.

Such unbidden services combat eloquence with sleep.

I witnessed the "Continuing Revelation"
poster on the ceiling as I screamed:

The plausibility of benefit through abuse questions the validity of consent!

I've
been having chest pains.

I Goofs Sometimes

or,

In the latest incident, I fled the house barefoot in the snow.

Sometimes God stomps his authority.

Woman was his house;
he paints his house with ice.

He comes to that era of frigid water
with retrieval
                    and forgetting

and possibly even dead trees.

That sweet little lady might just want to run and hide.

(Dear Animal-Assisted / Transitional Objects,
don't try to resist me. / I choose my favourites
based on family dynamics / portrayed in the motion
of classical madmen.)

She feels from one minute to the rest-
less climate issued by outbursts.

She hand-picks out-of-body health-risks
tempts nature to whip her
with windstorms
and dress her
in daring
drifts.

She deficits sleep to an uplifting trance
to cast glee through all the world!
Upon waking: Hello giggles!

But the added innerglow cannot penetrate ice.

Her soul plays out in the yard with longing:
Once Upon a Time Going Home.

Shadows stalk her as though she's been bad.

DON'T YOU SCREAM

"She'll get over it."

(Dear Fuzzy Set / of Universal Themes,
speak to my views on dysphoria.
I've led you through windows and tunnels
and pipes / to water / to just be condemned.)

God rarely bespeaks Himself.

But He was not raised in a whorehouse,
Nor did He lose a parent to cholera.

He was not sentenced to suicide,
Nor an invalidating home.

He absorbed no home-cooked goodness
through beat service or a lock-out.

No somnambulation through snowstorms
to the hospital for help.

No golddusting at Yellowstone
to pay a guy named Bear.

And He has no map of his drinking habits,
but He has eaten poorly for years.

Yet he sometimes transcends
his pervasive pattern of rimfire.

Disrupt,
Simply stump,
Look for easy prey

For finely honed,
Severely toned,
Artificially-made snow

Unexpected,
Empathy-cropped,
Characterological distortion

Of rural delights,
the gentle types:
animals and children.

He should've named the apple Norma Jean
and chopped down the tree
at the root.

(Dear Immaculate Congregate
within my Winter Wallpaper, / all thousands
of you critters and endless woodsy things,
Mother Nature does not listen to her parents.
I've steered you to serious danger.)

Her pioneering work, hardy for the zone,
includes being proactive and insightful
about each moodening int-eruption

through the deep
winter
soak
of sadness.

Underduck the nightmare of
f dread.
a
ll
on -chipping
his wood

Cast the magic of spring
and independent
study!

Pressure-cook summer
volcano's potions,
piss in every corner of the house.

(Of course, He had begun her education at home
with multiple motives:
manuals/depth charts,
obscure references
to entanglement,
the actor's
craft,
intentional vagueness,

And allowing

a great deal
less than
an hour

of snow play.

Not to mention a lapsed near-death holiday.)

(The gaps in scholarship were the Holy Spirit's way

of providing a security blanket

with the emotional depth

of the seven

dwarves.)

(Dear Farm Friends betwixt the Glory Dells,
Lonesome Crow and Restless Pup,
only half of you are practical:
those who are weak will die,
others camouflage and vanish.

Prepare yourselves to face the world.
Adopt your own skins now.)

(Dear Missmaster Wolf,
not even you can / doctor yourself
or your response to / the cover-up.

I must trust
that the standard of care
in your new tiny home / be humane

—Stuffed in the attic, 10 light-years away.)

Indeed.

With fun and with practice,
I can now ride my bike.

It's just a short jaunt up the hill.

I can also cook.
(Calling borderline crunchies.)
Gardening, too.

Natural music of the land!

When I'm in love:
the mushiest person.

The capability to be happy
All Day and All of Night.

dawn!
of
edge
the
to
rise
and
tree
any
climb
can
I

But sometimes...

...I goofs.

"Get over it."

Acknowledgments

My herd was always close to my heart during the writing of this. Emily, thank you for the decades of swimming through my sea of cockamamie musings. The big would die for the little. Andrea, I am grateful you're in our lives. Carla, you have been my faraway big sister, my window to the weird and wonderful; thank you for clearing a path for me in our family of origin. I write for Emma, Zoë, and Heidi's future. And for Oliver's. Our weekend moments of fun and silliness have seen me through many a week. Michael and Nicole, I appreciate every intersection of our lives, and I am blessed to have been sheltered by your strength. Wendy, I choose you for your unconditional love. You've chosen me, too, and I know you'll never turn me away. Wayne, my treasured chosen dad, whom we lost before this publication, thank you for your patience and acceptance of my twisted teenage brain. I'll always be your "Kiddo," but with your guidance, I grew. Most of all, Jefferey, my opener of doors. You feed me; you sustain me. I shudder to think where I would be without you. Plus, you're hilarious and adorable.

I remember with love and gratitude the many non-human animals who've shared their lives with me. Thank you to the cats I grew up with for their companionship; thank you to the dogs for their compassion. And, to Molly, whose pawprints pad beside me, and Boban, my wise retired soul, you took such good care of me while I was struggling, and shared with me so many joys. Gus, Survivor of the Battle, whom I had to say goodbye to during this process, you were my best friend and my own first. Claire-Blair, I eagerly anticipate your warmth on my lap during my next project. Kitty Tony Aster, you have persisted with me, and your permanent antics and happiness have brought me the balance needed to revisit past traumas.

Ada, our feminist wiles brought me here, and you are always in my heart. Steph, Adam, and Gilbert, I am so glad we found each other again. It means so much that you have supported our pack with your wisdom and selflessness. Ingrid, speaking of finding each other again... perhaps someday I will write our story. Everyone who has been a part of *S/tick*, this book would not have been born without you. I especially appreciate Repeat Defenders like Elaine Woo and Rachael Z. Ikins for making it a community. Katherine Davis, thank you for taking the risk to reach out to me. I value your contributions and friendship. I dearly appreciate the daily tea, giggles, and support from my colleagues from NQ, NAIT, and AU, and the inspiration from my students. I also acknowledge with gratitude the mentors who have kindled my creative endeavours (in alphabetical order by first name): Bonnie Ambrose, Clara Joseph, Emily Cargan, and Myron Dearden.

I have several old friends whom I must thank for allowing pieces of themselves to still nourish my heart. Neesha, my writing partner in crime, the merging of our imaginations not only solidified my love of writing but also offered me practical skills in the online world without which this book would not have come to life. Amanda, we remain kindred spirits, though you soul-searched long before me. And Kelsey, in particular: the piano still plays for you and your little ones. Mart and Ash, my two dear roommates from college days, I feel honoured that we glimpsed and withstood each other's ecstasies and anguish. My tiny dancer, I recall you with fondness and cherish the alternate universe where we skip hand-in-hand along the street while cowards in red trucks jeer at our queerness. Deb, I often miss you.

This book would not have been possible without the support of several generous donors. I would like to thank (in alphabetical order by first name) Amanda Foote, Carla Tree, Connor Coyne, Greg Goa, Ingrid Tenkate, Katherine Davis, Kent Cameron, and Wayne and Wendy Watt for their thoughtful contributions and faith in me. I also appreciate the contributions of 8 anonymous donors and Camellia Phillips, Charles Siegel, David Devoe, Emily Perkins-Harbin, James

Schirmer, Jan Worth-Nelson, Jessica Fogle, John Laycock, Kyle Edgeworth, Liesel Tarquini, Michael Wilson, Nick Simmons, Rachel Ziemba, Reinhardt Suarez, Rob Gilmor, Shannie Coyne, Veronica Howard, and Whitney Watt.

A deep thank you to Anastasia Walker, Emily Michaud, and Minnie Bruce Pratt for your kind and valued feedback on specific poems in this collection. Thank you of course to Jeff Watt for your guidance on and contributions to the cover art. To the blossoming team at Gothic Funk Press, please accept my warmest thank you for devoting your time and energy to turn this into something worth holding in your hands and reading. For catapulting GFP from its pupation without hesitation based on me approaching you with this work, I am truly indebted to Connor Coyne. For your valued expertise, I thank Jessica Coyne, Reinhardt Suarez, and Sam Perkins-Harbin. And, I never want to write another book without the immeasurable editorial insights of one Elisabeth Blair.

Finally, I would like to acknowledge the following authors and creators for the patches of their work that contributed to the found poetry process of "The Impersonal is Poclitical": Allacquére Rosanne Stone, Margaret Mitchell, Sue Townsend, and Susanna Forrest; as well as J. F. Beck; Christopher Dickey; Henry T. Gray, Thomas Pickering Pick and Robert Howden; Herman B. Hayes; Dennis Kucinich; John Leo; Trey Parker and Matt Stone; and Thomas Von der Osten-Sacken and Thomas Uwer.

About the author

Self-portrait of author

Sarah-Jean Krahn is the co-founder of *S/tick* and has acted as Managing Editor since its inception in 2012. She is passionate about feminist writing, especially that which flagrantly breaks from the norm in terms of both content and form. She is the author of *Weed Apologue* (words(on)pages, 2017), a chapbook about the intersections between colonization, the destruction of the earth, and violence against women. She hopes *A Girl Who Was His House* will inspire other writers and artists dis-eased by the patriarchy to (int)erupt the experimental literary cosmos with their traumas and resolutions.

Treaty 6 land is where Sarah-Jean gratefully resides. She shares a humble home with a beloved cat, dog, human, and snail in amiskwaciy-wâskahikan (Beaver Hill House), traditional meeting ground for many Indigenous nations, including the Cree, Saulteaux, Nakota Sioux, Blackfoot and Métis Peoples. Sarah-Jean has long worked as a student support in post-secondary education, aiming to inspire confidence and love of writing in those who struggle with it.

More from Sarah-Jean can be found at sarahjeancreates.com. *S/tick* and *Weed Apologue* can be read freely at dontdiepress.org.

Publication credits

Note: All poems have been edited or revised since their earlier publication.

"menarche" was previously published in *GUSH: Menstrual Manifestos for Our Times* (Frontenac House, 2019) and *ditch, poetry* (2013).

"Peaches" was previously published in *The Paramanu Pentaquark* by Gothic Funk Press (2016).

"No Privacy...but COOKIES!," "Seduction," and "Among Friends" were previously published in *Skidrow Penthouse* 18 (2015).

"Journal of Dead Bodies and Hidden Treasures" was previously published in *Bop Dead City* 8 (2014) and won best poem award for that issue.

Self-portrait of author was previously published as a portion of "Anarchical Borderline Child" in *Salon Style: Fiction, Poetry & Art* (New Lit Salon Press, 2014).

"A Tea Party in the Co-op Parking Lot" was previously published in *ditch, poetry* (2013).

"The Impersonal is Poclitical" was previously published in *Feminist Studies* 39.1 (2013).

"Symptomatology of an Impostor" was previously published in *This Assignment is So Gay* (Sibling Rivalry Press, 2013).

"Woman Messages" was previously published in *The Understanding between Foxes and Light* (great weather for MEDIA, 2013).

Made in the USA
Monee, IL
27 May 2021

68738844R00079